Great Big Animals

SUPERLONG ANACONDAS

By Charles M. Jones

Please visit our website, www.garethstevens.com. For a free color catalog of all our high-quality books, call toll free 1-800-542-2595 or fax 1-877-542-2596.

Cataloging-in-Publication Data

Names: Jones, Charles M.
Title: Superlong anacondas / Charles M. Jones.
Description: New York : Gareth Stevens Publishing, 2018. | Series: Great big animals | Includes index.
Identifiers: ISBN 9781538209158 (pbk.) | ISBN 9781538209172 (library bound) | ISBN 9781538209165 (6 pack)
Subjects: LCSH: Anaconda–Juvenile literature.
Classification: LCC QL666.O63 J66 2018 | DDC 597.96'7–dc23

First Edition

Published in 2018 by
Gareth Stevens Publishing
111 East 14th Street, Suite 349
New York, NY 10003

Editor: Kate Mikoley
Designer: Sarah Liddell

Photo credits: Cover, p. 1 MPF/Wikimedia Commons; pp. 5, 19, 24 (snake) Vadim Petrakov/Shutterstock.com; p. 7 Marcelina Zygula/Shutterstock.com; p. 9 Cromagnon/Shutterstock.com; p. 11 Claus Meyer/Minden Pictures/Minden Pictures/Getty Images; p. 13 Josve05a/Wikimedia Commons; p. 15 nounours/Shutterstock.com; pp. 17, 24 (spot) Jess Kraft/Shutterstock.com; p. 21 FOTOMIRO/Shutterstock.com; p. 23 Vladimir Wrangel/Shutterstock.com.

Printed in China

CPSIA compliance information: Batch #CW18GS: For further information contact Gareth Stevens, New York, New York at 1-800-542-2595.

Contents

Anacondas are huge snakes!

They are the biggest in the world.

Some weigh
550 pounds.

Some are 30 feet long.

Babies are about
2 feet long.

They eat other animals.

Some have bits
of white or black.
These are called spots.

Some live 10 years.

They live near water.

Anacondas love to swim.

Words to Know

snake

spot

Index